Scrambl

Heads

CU00852664

Text copyright © 2016 Emily Palmer

Illustration copyright © 2016 Emily Palmer

First published 2016. Printed in the UK.

Scrambled Heads

Text and illustrations by Emily Palmer

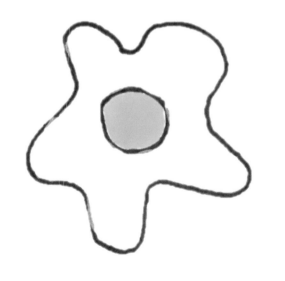

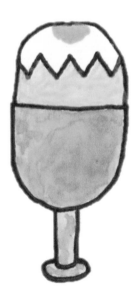

Life can be a lot of fun! There are so many great things to do.

But sometimes, we might have problems with our mental health. This is when our brain is poorly.

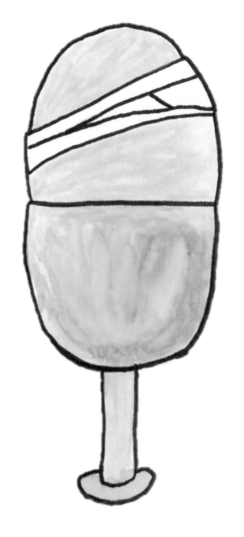

When we are poorly, we feel and act differently. This can affect how happy we are.

It can affect our thoughts and feelings, our mood, and our relationships with others.

Being poorly can be very scary when you don't feel like you have control over the things you think and feel.

When someone we love is poorly, we feel sad and we may be angry at the illness. It can be difficult to know what to say or do to help.

We want to help our loved one feel better again. There are many ways we can make things a little easier, but it is useful to talk about what could help.

When we are worried about how we are feeling, there are lots of people we can talk to. They can help us get more support if we need it.

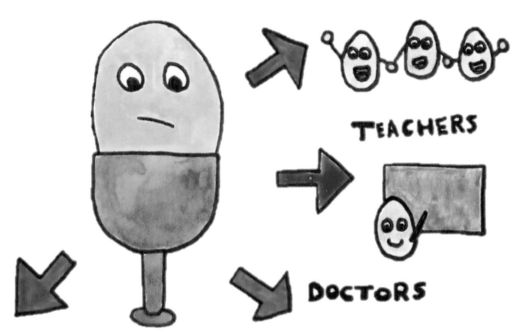

FRIENDS

TEACHERS

FAMILY

DOCTORS

There are lots of people who are trained to help us when we are poorly, we may get help from a special doctor who knows lots about mental health.

The special doctors can help us to open up and understand our thoughts and feelings.

We may visit them once or twice, or lots of times.

They might look after
us in a special hospital
if we need extra help.

In the hospital there are other people like us who are getting better too.

Even when we are ill, we look just like everyone else, so people may not see how unwell it makes us feel.

This does not make our illness any less real, but it can be harder for others to understand.

Whether we are healthy or poorly, it is important for us to love ourselves and each other.

Together, we are stronger!

10% of the profits from the first edition will be donated in support of YoungMinds.

Emily Palmer's own struggles as a child and young adult with her mental health inspired her to write a book to encourage awareness among children and families.

SCRAMBLED HEADS, her first children's book is described as "Utterly brilliant" by one mother and "One step closer to breaking the stigma of mental health" by another.

Emily hopes her book can fill a gap in the education of mental health, and start a dialogue on an issue that affects us all.